Sharks

and other Sea Creatures

DK

DK | Penguin Random House

Senior editor Carrie Love
Senior designers Hannah Moore, Lisa Robb
Designer Rachael Hare
Consultant John P Friel
Photographer Ruth Jenkinson
Pre-Production Producer Nikoleta Parasaki
Senior producer Isabell Schart
Jacket designer Amy Keast
Jacket coordinator Francesca Young
Managing editor Penny Smith
Managing art editor Gemma Glover
Art director Jane Bull
Publisher Mary Ling

First published in Great Britain in 2017 by
Dorling Kindersley Limited
80 Strand, London WC2R 0RL

A CIP catalogue record for this book is available
from the British Library.

ISBN: 978-0-2412-7438-5

Printed in China

Discover more at **www.dk.com**

Parents

This book is packed with activities
for your little ones to enjoy.
All projects are designed to have
an adult present. Please be safe
and sensible – especially when
you're doing anything that might
be dangerous (or messy!)
Have fun.

Contents

Who lives in the ocean?

It's not just **fish** that live in the **ocean**. There are reptiles, mammals, and invertebrates too.

Manta ray

Puffer fish

Blue marlin

Trumpet fish

Nassau grouper

Angelfish

Sea horse

Clownfish

Crab

See how many mammals, reptiles,

Mammals

are warm-blooded creatures like us. They drink milk from their mum when they're first born.

Reptiles

are covered with scales or hard shells, and they breathe through lungs.

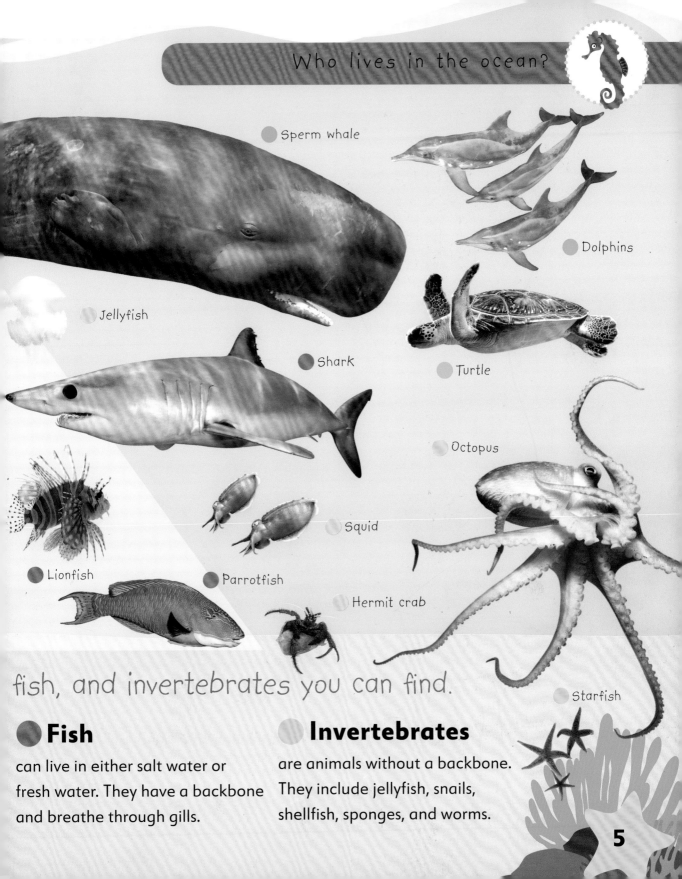

Sperm whale

Dolphins

Jellyfish

Shark

Turtle

Octopus

Squid

Lionfish

Parrotfish

Hermit crab

Starfish

fish, and invertebrates you can find.

Fish

can live in either salt water or fresh water. They have a backbone and breathe through gills.

Invertebrates

are animals without a backbone. They include jellyfish, snails, shellfish, sponges, and worms.

Big eaters

Sharks **eat** all kinds of animals, but they are mostly harmless to humans. They live in **oceans** all around the world.

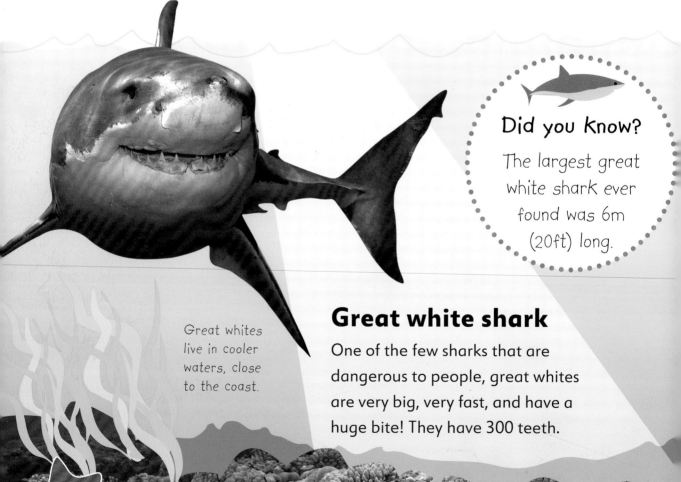

Did you know?

The largest great white shark ever found was 6m (20ft) long.

Great whites live in cooler waters, close to the coast.

Great white shark

One of the few sharks that are dangerous to people, great whites are very big, very fast, and have a huge bite! They have 300 teeth.

6

Biggest

Whale sharks are the biggest of all sharks. They can reach lengths of 12m (40ft).

Fastest

Mako sharks are the fastest sharks around. They can swim at a top speed of 97kph (60mph).

Fiercest

Tiger sharks are fearsome in their hunting style. They catch prey close to shore and will eat just about anything.

Hammerhead shark

These sharks are able to easily spot prey because the position of their eyes allows them to see in all directions at once.

Leopard shark

Leopard sharks get their name from the pattern on their skin. They eat clams, shrimp, worms, crabs, squid, and small fish.

7

Shark picture

Don't be frightened of this shark's face; he's more **startled** than scary! He's fun and easy to make.

Once you've completed your shark picture, you can frame it or give it away as a gift.

You will need:

Pencil
Coloured card
. Scissors
Glue
Tissue paper
Frame (optional)

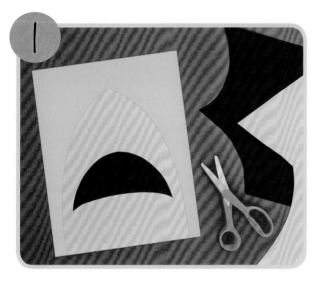

1

Draw a shape for the shark's head and mouth. Ask an adult to cut them out. Glue them onto a blue sheet of card.

2

Ask an adult to cut strips of *blue tissue paper*. Stick them onto the card in rows of light and dark *blue tissue paper*.

3

Draw *black* and *white* circles for the shark's eyes. Ask an adult to cut them out. Glue the eyes onto the picture.

4

Lastly, draw triangle shapes for the shark's teeth. Ask an adult to cut them out. Glue the teeth on the shark's mouth.

Coral fish

Coral **reefs** are home to lots of fish, and plants called anemones. These are a great place for clownfish to **hide** from their enemies.

Clownfish help the anemone as their poo acts as a fertilizer.

Did you know?

Clownfish aren't always orange and white. They can be yellow, black, or red, with white.

Sticky protection

Anemones can sting fish, but clownfish have a sticky layer of mucus that protects them. Clownfish hide in anemones to avoid enemies.

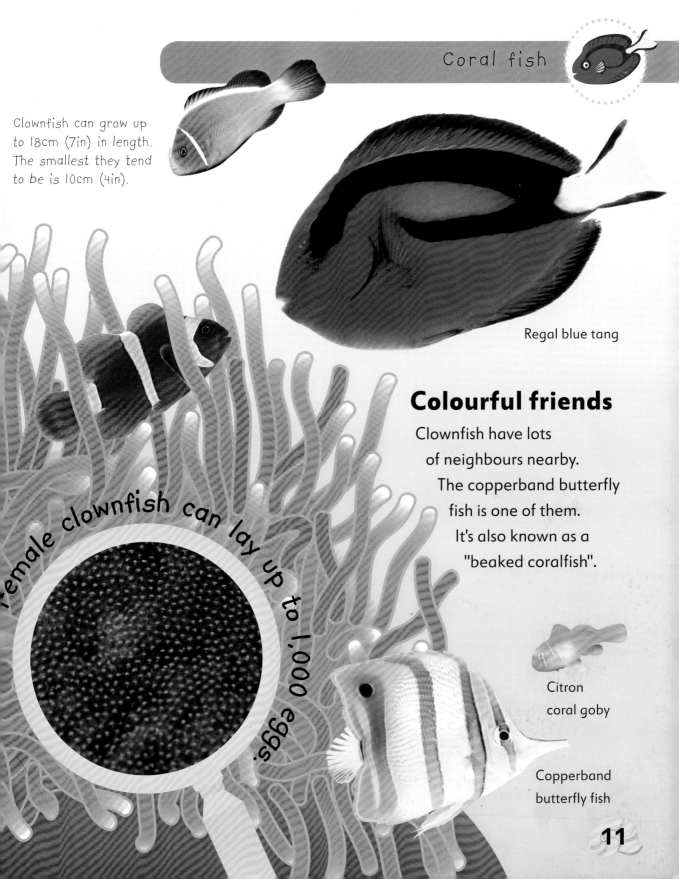

Clownfish can grow up to 18cm (7in) in length. The smallest they tend to be is 10cm (4in).

Regal blue tang

Female clownfish can lay up to 1,000 eggs.

Colourful friends

Clownfish have lots of neighbours nearby. The copperband butterfly fish is one of them. It's also known as a "beaked coralfish".

Citron coral goby

Copperband butterfly fish

11

Cool clownfish

Make a colourful **clownfish** for a fin-tastic ocean display!

You will need:

Pencil
Paper plates
Scissors
Tape
Paint and brushes
Googly eyes

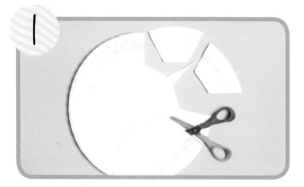

1 Draw two small wedge shapes for fins and a large one for a tail on a paper plate. Ask an adult to cut out the shapes.

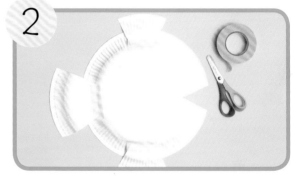

2 Tape the fins and tail to the back of another paper plate. Ask an adult to cut out a triangle for the fish's mouth.

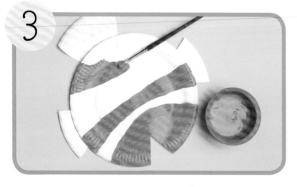

3 Flip over the plate. Paint orange stripes on the body. Paint the fins and the tail orange. Set aside to dry.

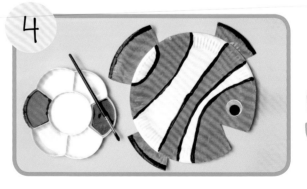

4 Paint thin black lines along the edges of the stripes, tail, and fins. When dry, stick on a googly eye to finish your fish!

Use different patterns and colours to make a whole sea of pretty fish.

13

Rainbow fish

These **bright**, colourful fish are very pretty to look at. Almost all of them live in warm and **shallow** waters.

Blue

Yellow

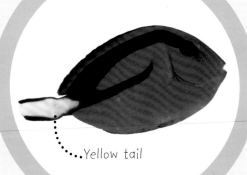

Yellow tail

Regal tangs turn blue as they age. When they're young they're bright yellow.

The **yellow tang** is bright yellow during the day, but at night, a brown and white patch appears on its body.

Close to coast

Colourful fish don't swim in very deep water. They prefer underwater caves, lagoons, and coral reefs.

The mandarinfish uses its bright colours to warn other animals not to eat it.

Orange

Black stripes

Male and female **flame angelfish** are difficult to tell apart as their colouring is so similar.

Purple and Yellow

The purple front half of a **royal gramma** actually appears to be blue when underwater!

Jellyfish

With a wobbly body and long **tentacles**, jellyfish look a bit like watery **blobs**! Jellyfish live together in groups called smacks.

Blue shining jellyfish

Strange swimmers

Jellyfish swim by opening and closing their bodies. When they do this, their bodies draw in water and then force it back out, which pushes them forward.

Light show

There are around 300 different species of jellyfish. They range in size from huge to tiny, and some types can glow in the dark!

Purple stinger
jellyfish

Blobby body

The soft, squidgy, see-through
body of a jellyfish is called the
bell. Long tentacles hang from
the bell. These tentacles can
sting, so stay away from them!

Pacific sea
nettle jellyfish

Did you know?

Jellyfish use their long
tentacles to stun and
catch food. They eat
small fish, shrimp, and
other jellyfish.

Australian
spotted
jellyfish

17

Jolly jellyfish

Make these **bright** jellyfish as decorations for your bedroom.

You will need:

Pencil, paper bowl, string, paint and brush, glitter glue, scissors, assorted ribbons and rick rack, tape, googly eyes.

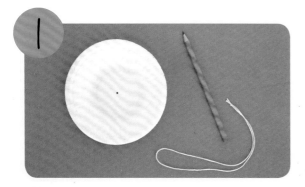

Ask an adult to use a pencil to make a hole in the centre of the paper bowl. Tie the string in the hole.

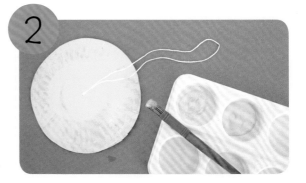

Paint the bowl and let it dry. Then paint the bowl with a layer of glitter glue. Set aside to dry.

Turn the bowl over. Ask an adult to cut the ribbons and rick rack. Tape them around the edges of the bowl.

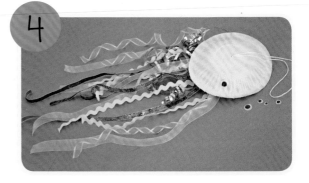

Turn the bowl right side up again and add the googly eyes to the jellyfish's face.

18

You can make a whole collection of jellyfish. Mix and match the colours if you like.

19

Super starfish

Although they're called starfish, these **amazing** creatures aren't even fish. For one thing, they can't even swim!

How many starfish can you count?

Did you know?
Starfish are also known as "sea stars".

Sticky feet on starfish's arms help them cling to rocks.

Starfish have an eye spot at the end of each arm.

6

4

7

5

1

3

2

8

20

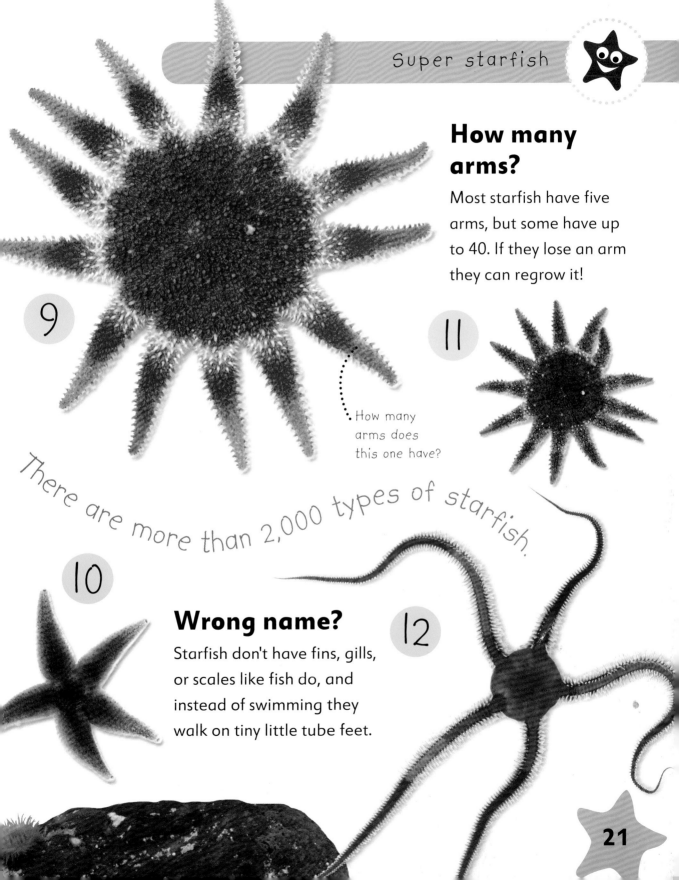

How many arms?

Most starfish have five arms, but some have up to 40. If they lose an arm they can regrow it!

9

11

How many arms does this one have?

There are more than 2,000 types of starfish.

10

Wrong name?

Starfish don't have fins, gills, or scales like fish do, and instead of swimming they walk on tiny little tube feet.

12

21

Puffer fish

A **slow**, **little fish** is an easy target for bigger fish, but the puffer fish has a **secret surprise** – it can puff up like a **balloon**!

Before

There are more than 100 types of puffer fish.

Before

Did you know?

There is stretchy skin on a puffer fish's stomach to help it grow and shrink.

Prickly fish

Many puffer fish have an extra layer of protection. They have spikes that stick out of their bodies.

22

Self defence

Puffer fish puff up to scare off predators. When it's inflated, it can't fit into a bigger fish's mouth! A puffer fish grows bigger by swallowing lots of water or air.

Spikes sticking out of it's body..........

After

A puffer fish is up to three times larger when puffed up!

After

Poison touch

Lots of puffer fish have toxic skin. This makes them dangerous to other animals in the sea.

23

Puffer fish painting

It's so much **fun** to make a **masterpiece** with **bright** colours and **plastic forks**.

Use your painting on the front of a greetings card for a birthday or other special occasion.

You will need:

Coloured card and pencil
Paints and brushes
Plastic forks
Sheets of black and white foam
Scissors
Glue

24

Draw a circle on the card. Paint the lower half of the circle using a fork dipped in white paint, making the edges spiky. Leave to dry.

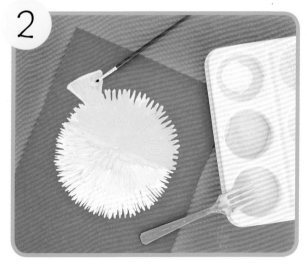

Make a yellow spiky circle, overlapping the white. Add fins with a paintbrush, and white lines when it's dry.

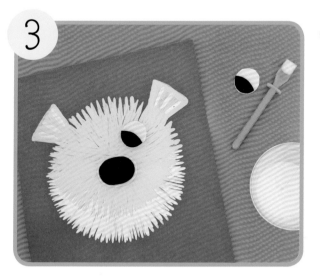

Ask an adult to cut out eyes and a mouth from the foam sheets as shown. Glue onto the picture.

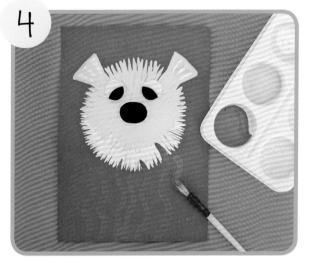

Finally, use a paintbrush dipped in green paint to create seaweed. It's just like you're on the sea floor!

Octopus maze

Octopuses are unusual animals. They have **three hearts**, eight arms, blue blood, and **no bones**. Some can even change colour!

Brain boxes

Octopuses are so clever that they can solve maze puzzles. Can you help the octopus on the next page escape from the maze?

If they feel threatened, octopuses spray ink to confuse their enemies.

Octopuses' arms are covered in suction cups that help them grip their prey.

26

Finish

Oops, this isn't the right way. There's a hungry **shark** looking for his next meal – turn back!

Lobsters are dinner for some species of octopus. Eat a quick meal then head back to the maze.

Start

Dolphins are one of the animals that prey on octopuses. Better spray ink at it and then escape back into the maze.

27

Pretty parrotfish

Parrotfish were given their name because of their tightly packed **teeth** that look like the beak of a parrot.

Home sweet home

Parrotfish eat the algae from the coral they live in, which stops the reef from being choked by greenery.

Did you know?

For protection at night, some parrotfish cover themselves in a mucus *bubble*.

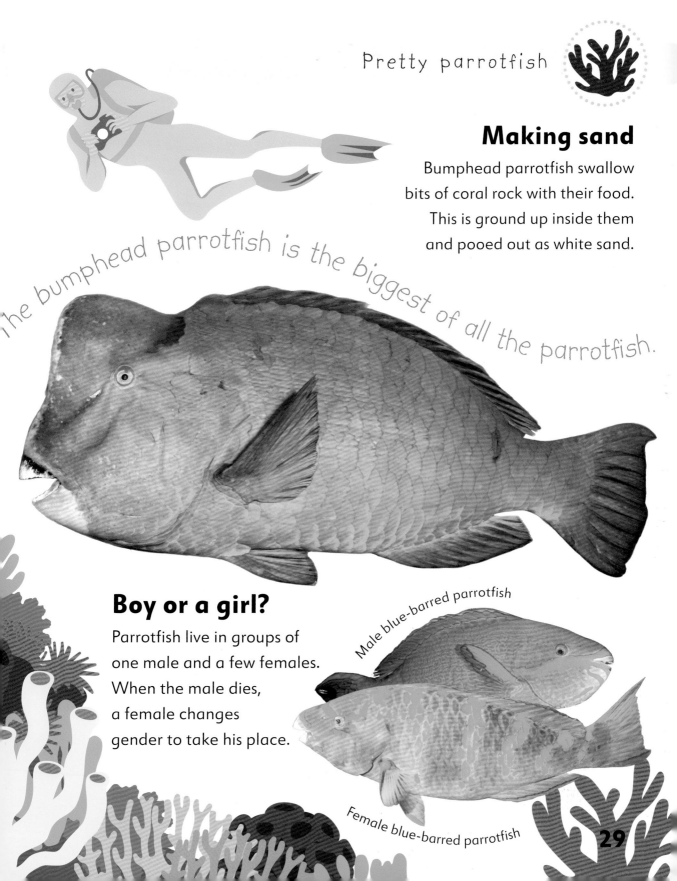

Making sand

Bumphead parrotfish swallow
bits of coral rock with their food.
This is ground up inside them
and pooed out as white sand.

The bumphead parrotfish is the biggest of all the parrotfish.

Boy or a girl?

Parrotfish live in groups of
one male and a few females.
When the male dies,
a female changes
gender to take his place.

Male blue-barred parrotfish

Female blue-barred parrotfish

Egg box ocean

Make your own **sparkly ocean scene** using an egg carton, colourful foam, and pretty shells.

You will need:

Egg carton, blue paint, paintbrush, glitter glue, blue chalk, scissors, sheets of pink, orange, and green foam, glue, shells, plastic gems.

Paint the egg carton blue and allow to fully dry. Add glitter glue and set it aside to dry. Then scribble on waves using the blue chalk.

Ask an adult to cut out fish shapes from the pink and orange foam. Stick the fish shapes in the top half of the inner carton.

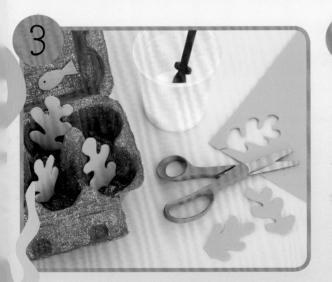

Ask an adult to cut seaweed shapes out of the green sheet of foam. Stick them into the bottom of the carton.

Glue in shells and add gems all over as a finishing touch.

Index

Acknowledgements

The publisher would like to thank the following for their kind permission to reproduce their photographs:
(Key: a-above; b-below/bottom; c-centre; f-far; l-left; r-right; t-top)
2 123RF.com: Eric Isselee (cb). Dorling Kindersley: Jerry Young (crb). 2-3 naturepl.com: Chris & Monique Fallows (c). 3 Alamy Stock Photo: Kevin Schafer (cla). 4 Alamy Stock Photo: David Wall (cb); Stephen Frink Collection (clb). Fotolia: uwimages (cb/anemonefish). naturepl.com: Alex Mustard (crb); Pascal Kobeh (cra). 4-5 naturepl.com: Doug Perrine (t). 5 Dorling Kindersley: Linda Pitkin (clb). naturepl.com: Brandon Cole (cl); Michael Pitts (cla); Doug Perrine (cra). 6 naturepl.com: Mark Carwardine (cl). 6-7 naturepl.com: Alex Mustard (b). 7 Dorling Kindersley: Jerry Young (clb). naturepl.com: Brandon Cole (ca); Doug Perrine (cla, cra); Chris & Monique Fallows (c). 10 123RF.com: Brian Kinney (tr); Eric Isselee (clb); mexrix (cb). 11 123RF.com: Christopher Waters (clb); Olga Khoroshunova (tc); Eric Isselee (cla). Dorling Kindersley: Jerry Young (cra); Linda Pitkin (crb). 16 Alamy Stock Photo: Westend61 GmbH. 17 Alamy Stock Photo: Kevin Schafer (cr). naturepl.com: Elaine Whiteford (l); Michael Pitts (br). 22 Dorling Kindersley: Jerry Young (cr). 23 Alamy Stock Photo: Tsuneo Nakamura / Volvox Inc (b). 26 Alamy Stock Photo: Blickwinkel. 27 123RF.com: Jennifer Barrow / jenifoto (crb); Sergey Nivens / nexusplexus (br). Fotolia: Rolffimages (cla). 28 Dorling Kindersley: Linda Pitkin (cla). FLPA: Reinhard Dirscherl (br). 29 Dorling Kindersley: Linda Pitkin (c). FLPA: Colin Marshall (crb/Parrotfish); Fred Bavendam / Minden Pictures (crb). 32 123RF.com: Eric Isselee (cb). Dorling Kindersley: Linda Pitkin (crb). Fotolia: uwimages (bc). naturepl.com: Brandon Cole (tr). Cover images: Back: Dreamstime.com: Secondshot clb

All other images © Dorling Kindersley
For further information see: www.dkimages.com

Dorling Kindersley would also like to thank James Mitchem for editorial assistance, Sophia Danielsson-Waters and Helene Hilton for proofreading.